A Quite Misunderstood Religion

Kevin Micuch

Charleston, AR:
COBB PUBLISHING
2020

A Quite Misunderstood Religion is copyright 2020 © Kevin Micuch. All rights reserved.

No part of this book may be reproduced in any way (whether print, audio, digital, electronic, or any other means) without the expressed written permission of the author.

Published in the United States of America by:

Cobb Publishing
704 E. Main St.
Charleston, AR 72933
www.CobbPublishing.com
CobbPublishing@gmail.com
479.747.8372

ISBN: 978-1-947622-48-7

Contents

"Christianity is a Blind Faith" 5

"The Bible Contains Contradictions" 12

"The Bible Condones Slavery and Killing" 29

"Christianity Was Copied from Past Religions" 39

"You Believe in a Zombie!" 54

"Christians Are Too Judgmental" 62

"Most Wars Have Been in the Name of Religion" 68

"The Church" 73

Conclusion 83

What is truth? Truth has many different meanings to many different people. The word 'truth' is defined, though, as "a fact that has been verified" or "conformity with reality or actuality." Many, many people misunderstand this for some reason. Truth is basically, what is.

Many people in today's society, though, don't believe truth is real. You might hear someone say something like, "truth is relative" or "truth isn't the same for everyone." Some might even say they don't believe in truth at all. One person I asked said, "Truth is not universal. Truth is our reality, our perception. What we perceive to be real and honest. It is usually linked to a religious or moral concept."

As we can see, truth is getting misconstrued these days. Many link truth to our own perception of the world, whether it has to do with our religious beliefs, politics, or just our personal opinion about the world around us. This is why people can say and believe things like "truth is relative." Of course, it is when everyone has differing opinions on things. But what this new wave of thinking has done is actually redefined the term to suit their wants.

Let's go back to our definition. Truth is conforming to reality. It's not even dependent on our knowledge of it. Truth just *is*. Truth exists whether we want it to or not. To say truth doesn't exist is to say reality doesn't exist (some actually do). If you believe this, then this book might not be for you.

I choose to believe in reality. I believe truth exists because we can see it. Things like math, logic, and science are truth. Truth is absolute. Axioms like 3+3=6 and the law of the excluded middle are self-evident and true. The law of gravity keeps us from hitting the ceiling or walls every morning we get out of bed. Our feet hit the floor *every time*. These laws have been put into place by a Creator. I mean, think about it. To say "truth doesn't exist" is actually self-refuting. It's illogical. That statement would have to be true in order to be valid!

Even in everyday life, we want to know the truth. We want to know the exact amount that's in our bank account or what time our flight leaves or who ate the last cookie in the jar. However, when it comes to religion, somehow "truth is relative." How does that make sense? In religion, just like everything else, we ought to be searching for the truth. Weigh all of the options and draw the best conclusion. For me, I found that conclusion to be Christianity. That is what's involved in seeking for truth.

I chose to start with defining truth because that is going to be the foundation that I build upon. To reiterate, if you don't believe in truth, what is the point in believing anything? There would be no right or wrong. Everyone could just believe whatever they wanted. Someone could believe the sky is red, or even whipped cream. See how ridiculous that sounds? I hope now we can at least agree that truth does, in fact, exist. If falsehoods exist, truth must too. This book is for the truth seekers out there. Those who actually care about knowing what the truth is. Separating truth from the many lies. That is the point I'm trying to make.

Being a Christian, in this day and age, I see many on the outside misunderstanding what Christianity is all about. Probably even some on the inside, too. I pray I can shed some light on some of the issues skeptics of Christianity bring up.

For some reason, many today don't want to study things out for themselves. It's gotten easier to just believe what someone else has said. Those who oppose Christianity are going to say whatever they want about it. Mostly lies, of course. This is why I think Christianity has been getting a bad reputation. It's because we don't take the time to search things out for ourselves.

With that being said, here are some of the biggest accusations I've found against Christianity. I'm sure we could list a ton more, but I hope these more popular ones will suffice. Please, come along as we journey together in searching out the truth.

"Christianity is a Blind Faith"

I'd like to start with the accusation I've probably seen most often. That is that theists just have a blind faith. You can't prove a creator exists and so why believe in one? It's simply absurd to believe in something you can't perceive, right? Well, let's take a look.

If you were to look up the word *faith* in a dictionary, one definition you would find says, "a firm belief in something for which there is no proof." In a society that seems to be drifting away from God and wants nothing to do with the supernatural, this seems like the most appropriate definition. Those who have any kind of faith in a god of any sort are mocked and ridiculed by those who think they don't need any kind of faith in anything. These "free-thinkers," as they liked to be called, want to be freed from any kind of religion and higher authority. Famous atheist, Bertrand Russell, defines free thinking this way, "what makes a freethinker is not his beliefs but the way in which he holds them. If he holds them because his elders told him they were true when he was young, or if he holds them because if he did not, he would be unhappy, his thought is not free; but if he holds them because, after careful thought he finds a balance of evidence in their favor, then his thought is free, however odd his conclusions may seem." Such is the case with most that hold to this view.

So, if you had to be taught anything you are not a free thinker. That seems kind of silly don't you think? All knowledge must then be from self-learning, from what you perceive the world to be. This isn't always the case, though, as this would make things like school insignificant. You wouldn't be able to learn anything from anybody other than yourself. There would be no need for teachers in any capacity. You couldn't have, say, a mentor or life coach either. This just isn't how society works and it's sad that over time, the evolution of this word has come to mean something it doesn't.

Christianity is different though. Jesus knew that His teachings were dissentient among the majority. Not too many people agreed with what He preached, and because of that, He knew His followers would be hated (John 15:18) and persecuted (Luke 21:12; John 15:20) as well. Such was no different from past speakers of God (Deuteronomy 30:7; Daniel 7:25; Matthew 5:12; Acts 7:52). The Bible tells us that God's ways are not like the ways of the world (Isaiah 55:8). The world doesn't like God's ways and will do anything to suppress them.

A Christian's faith is also quite different from the way the world sees faith. The biblical definition of *faith* can be found in Hebrews 11. The first verse says "Now faith is the substance of things hoped for, the evidence of things not seen." We can plainly see, belief in God is grounded in evidence, not based on the lack thereof. Everyone should believe in the Creator because of the evidence He has provided for us (Romans 1:20-21). A Christian has faith because of what they have heard from the Bible. Christianity is not and has never been a "blind faith" or leap in the dark.

God has never wanted us to believe in something we weren't sure about. Jesus taught and performed miracles in order to prove what He was saying. In fact, the Greek word that is usually translated "faith" in Scripture is the word *pistis*. The definition of this word is "conviction of the truth of anything, belief." Therefore, anyone who believes in God does so in light of the evidence that has been presented to them.

Logically speaking, we can see this in our English word too. In order to believe in something, one would need ample evidence to back up their claim. Otherwise, it's simply seen as a hunch or gut feeling which requires no evidence whatsoever. We have faith or trust in someone or something because they have proven to be trustworthy. It would be ridiculous to trust in someone

A Quite Misunderstood Religion

blindly. Not to say you couldn't, but the point is that it usually requires evidence.

I want us to look at a couple of examples from Scripture. At the end of Exodus 4, we see the Israelites "believed" what Moses and Aaron were saying (v. 31). Why did they believe them? Because of the words that were spoken to them and the signs that were given to them (v. 30). They concluded from the evidence they were shown that what Moses and Aaron were saying was true.

Likewise, in the New Testament, many believed in Jesus' teachings. At what point did they believe? When they saw the signs He did (John 2:23; 11:45; 20:29). These people heard the teachings of Christ and saw the evidence of the miracles He gave to them and many believed Him because of it. The same as with the apostles after Jesus ascended into Heaven. They had preached Jesus to the people (Acts 2:38; 8:12-13; 9:41-42; 13:12, 48; 14:1; 18:8; Romans 10:17) who then believed and were baptized. Their belief was grounded in the evidence that was presented to them. In this day and age however, we don't have the signs and wonders they did back in those days. The miracles that happened back then were only to prove to those people that what was being said was from God. We now have these things in writings from these eyewitnesses to help show us what they saw back then and why they believed the Lord (John 20:30-31). The miracle today is shown within the pages of the Bible. It tells us about the life of Jesus, the death of Jesus, and the resurrection of Jesus and explains why He came to Earth.

This concept is further demonstrated in the fact that God actually commands us *not* to believe everything we hear. Instead, we are to "test the spirts" (1 John 4:1) and "prove all things" (1 Thessalonians 5:21). The Greek word in both verses is *dokimazo* and it means to test or examine something to see if it's genuine. Again, showing that what we believe is because we've examined the proof of the matter.

God has never expected us to believe in things blindly. He knows truth. He *is* truth (John 14:6). To seek after truth is to seek after God. The mere fact that truth exists proves God exists, for chaos cannot sustain itself.

It is not the purpose of this book to sit and list all of the evidences we've found for the existence of God, the validity of the Bible, and the reality of a man named Jesus of Nazareth. However, we do know that there are many writings, from both believers and objectors, that describe this Man that people worshiped and who was crucified under Pontius Pilate. Even the Jewish Talmud mentions this historical event. The question then becomes, was Jesus really who He claimed to be? I believe so.

"The Bible Contains Contradictions"

A Look at Logic

This is probably the accusation you'll hear most by skeptics about the Bible. This section has a lot to unpack, so this might be the longest chapter in this book. To start, I want to talk about logic. Logic can be defined as "the science that investigates the principles governing correct or reliable inference." The key phrase in this definition would be "correct or reliable." In other words, it's the best possible answer in a given situation. In math, if you were to say that 3+3=8, you would be in error. Well logic, like science, math, etc. has laws that one needs to use in order to properly apply it. These laws are absolute truths. This means, whatever way you look at it, it will stand true every time. Anything else would be false.

We use logic in our everyday lives, such as "which route to work would be the quickest?" In answering multiple choice questions, you might use the 'process of elimination' method. These are just some of the ways to use rational thinking each day, but can we use this when reading the Bible? Seeing as the Bible is just like any other book, why wouldn't we use logical thinking? We've been given a brain to use wisely, right? Why wouldn't we want to use it to read about God and understand what His will is for us?

Let's start with an example. Christians will say that there is only one church, yet you will not find this phrase anywhere in Scripture. How do they come up with such a conclusion? Well, we read in Ephesians 4:4 that there is only one body, that of our Lord. Going back to chapter 1 of the letter, we read in verses 22 and 23 that the body of

Christ is the church of Christ. These two are one in the same. So, using the logical equation 'if a = b and b = c, then a = c,' we can conclude that since there is only one body, there must only be one church.

Another example can be found in Genesis 13:1. We see that Lot returned to Canaan with Abram (Abraham) from Egypt. However, nowhere does it say that Lot was in Egypt. If one were to use rational thinking though, with the information that is given, they would have to conclude that Lot was in Egypt prior to this statement.

Look at Romans 1:20 also. Paul says that the invisible things of God can be seen with a clear perspective. The Greek word for *perceived* means to perceive with the mind. See, the human brain can do some extraordinary things. We know because it came from a divine Source.

One last example we could look at is Mark 16:16. It is clearly stated that belief (in Christ) and baptism are both necessary in order for one to receive salvation. Logically then, one would conclude that if one is not baptized and does not believe, they will not be saved. This is exactly what is said in the latter part of that verse. Here, the "baptized" is implied and not necessary to be reiterated because one will not be baptized if they do not believe.

Moving along, logic can also be used when dealing with the alleged contradictions that many claim are within the pages of the Bible. In logic, the law of contradiction basically states that "something cannot both be and not be." We cannot just assume that two verses contradict each other just because they might seem that way at first glance. There is a process one must use in order to determine if there is a contradiction or not, and the contexts of each verse will help you decide that. There are three methods to proving that two or more things are not a contradiction.

The first method to take would be to determine if the same subject is being talked about. If a novice to Scripture were to read about Noah's ark and then turn to a passage that talks about people carrying the ark (2 Samuel 15:25), they might ask themselves, "how could they carry such a large ship?" Well, when studied, one would come to the conclusion that it is two different arks being portrayed. The term *ark*, like many terms in the Bible, is used in different ways. We need to remember to let the context of a given passage define the term and not assume they are all the same.

Another example would be the word *works*. Many, even those who claim to be Christians, seem to not be able to comprehend this word. In the New Testament, there are different types of works that can be alluded to. There are works of the law (old law of Moses; Romans 3:28). There are works of human merit (Titus 3:5). There are also works of God (John 6:27). These do not contradict each other, as they are being used in a different capacity.

The second method would be to decipher if the same subject is being talked about *in the same time frame*. In the premise: "*Gary is rich; Gary is poor*," Gary could have been at one point rich and now is poor, or vice versa. These don't necessarily contradict because a different time frame could have been portrayed. We would have to know the contexts in order to make that decision.

The third method to take would be to see if the same subject is being talked about in the same time frame *and in the same sense*. In the premise: "Gary is tall; Gary is short," it could mean that Gary is tall in height, but short on money. Different words have different meanings to them, so again, it's the context that will reveal the meaning of the words being used. If all of these three steps come out positive, it is then, and *only then*, that we would have a contradiction. However, the Bible is free of contradictions.

I urge you to use the brain that God gave you. Use it wisely and not to simply listen to others and what they have to say. Much like I established a foundation of truth for this book, this discussion needed a foundation about logic because a lot of people like to twist words and their meanings. Only when we're searching for truth, will the truth be revealed.

Kevin Micuch

A Study on Supplementation

In addition to logic, I need also explain supplementation. It simply means to add to something. When the police are called to the scene of a crime, one of the first things they do is ask any witnesses what they saw. It would be ridiculous for them to only ask one witness for their testimony and then call it quits. They have to ask as many witnesses as they can to try and piece together what actually happened. Each witness' testimony supplements the others like a jigsaw puzzle to show the big picture.

This is exactly what the Bible does. We aren't given the full picture so we're reading many different written testimonies of what they saw. In the gospels for instance, we have four witness accounts to the life of Jesus. Just like the crime scene, we have four accounts that piece together the stories of our Lord and Savior. Some of these stories are the same, but with some of them you cannot get the full picture unless you read more than one account. One example would be the story of Peter cutting of the ear of the high priest's servant (Matthew 26:50-54; Mark 14:46-49; Luke 22:49-51; John 18:10-11). Each one of these passages supplements the other. They all give a piece of the story and it's only when you put them all together that you can see the whole picture.

Now, skeptics of the Bible will look at these statements and say that these don't supplement each other, but rather contradict one another. This is far from the truth. These verses do not contradict one another for they do not possess any contradictory information. For that to happen, they would have to be giving opposite information about the same things, at the same time, in the same sense; just like we learned in the previous section. To reiterate, the law of contradiction states that something cannot both *be* and *not be*. So, supplementary information does not contradict because it is just giving different perspectives of the same event.

Most Christians will realize this and claim that the whole Bible needs to be read in order to get the whole context. Yet, for some reason, they aren't consistent in their thinking. To further illustrate this, many

Christians today believe in what is called the 'faith only' doctrine. This is the belief that all you need to do in order to be saved is have faith. That is it. What they fail to do, however, is read the other verses which tell us about the other things that save us.

Now, I am not saying that faith doesn't save us. The Bible is pretty clear that it does (John 3:16; Ephesians 2:8; 1 Corinthians 1:21). What I am asserting is that it is not *just* faith that saves us. What the believers of this doctrine will do is pick out verses that only mention 'faith' or 'believe,' while ignoring the rest of the Bible—and that's just not proper hermeneutics. God also tells us that repentance saves us (Luke 13:3, 5; Acts 17:30; 2 Peter 3:9). Logically then, if we do not repent of our sins, we cannot be saved. Likewise, God also tells us that baptism saves us (Mark 16:16; Acts 2:38; 1 Peter 3:21). Paul even tells us that our hope saves us (Romans 8:24). So, if we do not do these things, there is no salvation for us. There are more saving verses, but I think you can see my point. All of these verses supplement one another. We cannot on one hand, ridicule the unbelievers for taking passages out of their biblical contexts and on the other hand, do it ourselves. It is hypocritical.

Alleged Contradictions

Now that I've established our foundations, I want to show you what I mean with some examples of alleged contradictions people throw out there. I could write a whole book on these, but I'll just give three examples. The first one, I tend to see a lot. It deals with the death of Judas Iscariot, the betrayer of Jesus. You can find these in Matthew 27:1-10 and Acts 1:15-19. One says that Judas hanged himself; the other says he burst open in the middle of a field. Many skeptics look at this and say they contradict because it is two different accounts of one man's death.

To start, let us recall our three methods to finding a contradiction. It is clear that we're talking about the same person so let's move on to the second method; timing. We're not really given the timing of the two incidents and really if you look at the verse in Acts, it doesn't even say that's how he died. Luke simply says that his intestines fell out. So, why can't these two passages supplement one another? Could it not be that both happened? I would say yes. Too, if you think about it scientifically, he could have hanged himself, then the chief priests brought the corpse out into a field where his intestines burst open. The gases that build up in the body postmortem certainly could have caused this, where vultures and other things would have eaten him. Therefore, I see no contradiction here.

Another popular example we can look at is the story of the Jesus' resurrection. It was a Sunday morning and Matthew wrote that *"Mary Magdalene and the other Mary came to see the tomb"* (28:1). An angel of the Lord appeared to them and said that Jesus was no longer there and to tell their friends. Then Mark writes in his gospel account that *"Mary Magdalene, Mary the mother of James, and Salome bought spices, that they might come and anoint Him"* (Mark 16:1). The angel tells them all that Jesus has risen and to go and tell others. Luke then records *"...[and the women who had come with Him from Galilee] and certain other women with them, came to the tomb bringing the spices which they had prepared*" (Luke 24:1). He later names Mary Magdalene, Joanna, and Mary, the mother of James and includes "other women." He then writes that it was two angels that told the women the Lord had risen and to go spread the news. And at last, John writes in his account, "*Mary Magdalene went to the tomb early, while it was still dark, and saw that the stone had been taken away from the tomb*" (20:1). And he doesn't even mention who told her that the Lord had risen. So, we have four different witness accounts of the same event. Who are we to believe?

Well, let's go back and see if these stories are just pieces of a puzzle. Could it be that these all supplement each other? Remember, these are four different accounts. They could just be telling the story from secondhand accounts. Perhaps they were only mentioning the women they knew. Maybe it was unbeknownst to Matthew and Mark of the other women traveling with the two Mary's. We may never know. What we do know is that a lot of women went to go see Jesus and He wasn't there. Two angels appeared and told them to tell the other disciples that Jesus had been resurrected.

We also know that the Bible doesn't give every detail to every account of every story. Yes, we cannot go beyond what is written. We can only speculate. But it's also foolish to simply claim that something is a contradiction without knowing all of the details first. What's good about logic and searching these things out is that you only need one possible explanation for it *not* to be a contradiction. Even if that one possibility isn't all that clear, it's still enough to dismiss the title of "contradiction." Ask any policeman and they will tell you that it actually raises more red flags when each witness has the exact same testimony than when there are variances. It's okay to have variances. A variance is not a contradiction.

One last example can be those that have "seen" God. There have been a couple of times where people are said to have seen God. A couple of examples would be Jacob (Genesis 32:30) and Moses (Exodus 33:21-

23). However, we also read verses like Exodus 33:20 and John 1:18 about people not being able to see God. So, which is it?

With this one, it's a matter of just reading what is being said. People like to make things out to something that's not there. You'll notice that Exodus 33 is shown on both sides. Here, God tells Moses that he can't see His face but He can see His "glory." He adds that Moses could even see His "back." The Bible doesn't give much more than that, so to go beyond what has been revealed is again just speculation.

No one is able to see God's true nature. John 4:24 tells us that God is a spirit. Being physical beings, we literally cannot even begin to visualize what a spirit is. That being said, spirits have taken temporal, physical bodies, both angels and demons. God has done this too, like in the story of Jacob in Genesis 32. He also took the form of the man we call Jesus. This is what it could mean to have *seen* God. And remember too, that words can have different meanings. Such can be said for "see" as well.

This is why logic is so important. If you've never studied logic before, I highly recommend it. Not just the Bible, but in other writings, you won't just blindly accuse it of containing a contradiction like many do today. But you will know how to figure out if there is one.

You also won't fall for silly questions that deniers of a creator bring up. The one I see quite often goes something like, "could God create a boulder so massive that even he couldn't lift it?" Such is just an illogical question. It doesn't even make sense. God operates by being true. By being logical. He cannot contradict Himself because truth doesn't contradict itself. Remember, He *is* truth. Yes, there are things that God cannot do because He is bound by His nature. An example would be He cannot sin because He is holy.

So, I hope now you can use these tools you've learned and decipher if something is contradictory or not. When we use them properly, we'll see that these discrepancies that skeptics bring up are, in fact, not contradictory at all because we know the Bible doesn't have any contradictions.

One last point, this can also apply to numbers that are recorded. A lot of these discrepancies people have found have to do with different numbers that have been written down. An example of this would be in John 20:24 where Thomas is named "one of the twelve" and yet Judas had already hung himself. At this moment in time, there were only eleven apostles.

We have to keep in mind figurative language. Just like today, people back then used figurative language to make a point. Not everything is to be taken literally or else yes, you would have a book full of contradictions. Remember, words can have different meanings and things can be conveyed figuratively as well. With the above example, the apostles that traveled with Jesus were simply called "the twelve." John could have simply recorded the title rather than the actual number of them. An example today would be us using the term "2 by 4" for some lumber. We know it's actually not 2x4 but it's just the title it's been given.

In addition, the Hebrews and Greeks didn't use the Arabic numbers we do today. Their numbers were a lot more intricate and complex. Even an extra line drawn or not drawn could have caused readers to interpret two different numbers. We can't hold these discrepancies as contradictions simply because they might have been translated incorrectly.

So, as we can see, the Bible does not contain any contradictions. Even as a compilation of writings spanning over two thousand years, it contains none. If that's not evidence of Intelligent inspiration, I don't know what is.

"The Bible Condones Slavery and Killing"

It saddens me when people try to change our culture's history to suit a more politically correct world. One of these changes is claiming the Confederate flag is a symbol of racism and slavery; therefore, it should be removed from the public eye. We have even taken it a step further and have cancelled reruns of the show 'Dukes of Hazzard' because the hood of the car bears this flag on it.

I can understand where people are getting offended by things like slavery. However, it's part of American history. It used to happen and now it doesn't. We cannot change the past so we need to leave it there and look forward to the future. This flag was never meant to symbolize racism. A flag is an inanimate object and therefore cannot show any emotion. Even if it were to symbolize anything, most people who display it said it simply symbolized pride. This could be said with any flag around the world. Those who choose to present a flag of any sort, only do so to show they are proud of where they came from.

With that being said, we cannot help with how people use such icons. I'm sure there were people using it for racism. We need to gear that anger towards the people though, not the symbol. Take the Holocaust for instance. Many today associate the swastika with Adolf Hitler and his Nazi regime. But what people may not know is that this symbol actually means peace, life, and good luck. Mr. Hitler actually flipped it around and rotated it a little to use it for the evil he executed. To some though, they may think that the swastika means anti-Semitism when it really doesn't. Simply how the symbol is used is where it gets its meaning from.

A Quite Misunderstood Religion

As for many people today, this becomes even a stumbling block to becoming a Christian. Those who oppose Christianity claim that the Bible itself condones things like slavery, and thus disregard it without giving the Bible a second look. Being a believer in the Bible, I would have to agree that the Bible does talk about slavery of all types. However, when we actually read what it says, it's far from what the skeptics are saying.

I've heard this claim numerous times, but the first thing that should be said is that just because the Bible mentions words like 'slave' or 'slavery' does not mean that God condones it. In fact, nowhere does it ever say that God condones slavery. We are all made in His image (Genesis 1:27) and we are all commanded to love one another (John 13:34). No one is better than anyone else, for we are all created equal. None of us are perfect, either. We all have sin in our lives (Romans 3:23) and are in need of a Savior. We are all on the same playing field in this regard.

So then, what does the Bible actually say about slavery? Is it like the 17th century "white man" slavery that it always gets compared to? Hardly. Sure, there were many civilizations that had owned slaves back in those times. It was a common practice to own slaves in days past, both Bible times and later. That's just how these civilizations operated. One of the most popular examples was the Israelites over in Egypt (Exodus 1). We have to remember, though, that many of these ancient civilizations were not believers in the one true God. Those who believed in Jehovah were to treat the situation a little differently.

Take a look at Leviticus 25 for example. Starting in verse 39, we see that many of the "slaves" the Jews had, *sold themselves* into it. If they needed some money, they basically worked for their "master." In that case, the same could be said today. I could say I'm a slave, in a sense, to my employer. I show up and do what I'm told and they pay me to work. They are my master in this sense.

A Quite Misunderstood Religion

The same can go for Christians. Those who choose to follow Christ and take up their cross daily have freely chosen that servitude. The apostle Paul often describes himself as a servant (Romans 1:1; Philippians 1:1; Titus 1:1). We see that it was not against their will, but they accepted God's saving grace and the blood of His Son to cleanse their souls. This is the complete opposite of what the 21st century American culture deems as "slavery," because the word has different meanings than just owning a human being. If it makes anyone feel better, I can use the word *servant* over the word *slave*.

Another thing we notice when we take the time to read Scripture is how these servants were treated in God-fearing communities. Going back to Leviticus 25, verses 43 and 46 tell the Israelites that if they did have servants, they were "not to rule over them with rigor." Here, the Hebrew word for *rigor* means "harshness, cruelty." So, even the servants were to be treated respectfully, like a brother or sister. They were not to be treated unfairly or as animals. They were not to be beaten or abused in any way. In addition, these servants were to be let go once their debt was paid.

We see this in Christian times, too. When Paul wrote to his friend Philemon, he told him to receive his servant Onesimus as a brother in Christ because he had been saved. Remember we are all one in Christ Jesus (Galatians 3:26-29). We are all members of one body, His church.

So, as we can see, God has never told His people to own any other human being. I don't believe anyone has that right to do so. This could just be the 21st century American in me though. But again, we are all on the same playing field. Many nations did so, as was custom in that day. That's just what they did. Yes, some were cruel to their servants and some weren't. I cannot change what they did. Those who were servants though, according to the Judeo-Christian God, were not treated any differently than non-servants. I'm just thankful many nations across the world now have abolished it completely.

This brings me now to the "killing" portion of this accusation. Another stumbling block for many is the fact that God killed and had His people kill many, many people in the Old Testament. For many, they see Christians speak about a loving God and see Jesus' character and then see the "God of old" who commanded mass genocide. They don't know how to deal with it, and for most, it turns them off completely.

So, is it true? Yes. We can read about such things in passages such as Deuteronomy 7:1-5. Here, God instructs the Israelites to destroy a nation if it tells you to go and serve other Gods. But, why would God command that?

For people interested in the truth, they would actually look for the answers and find them. Again, God will be found to those that are actually seeking Him (Psalm 22:26; Jeremiah 29:13; Lamentations 3:25). When we search it, we see that the underlying cause of this was sin. He is judging these nations because of their wickedness and He's simply using the Israelites to carry it out. He also does it Himself as we see with Sodom and

Gomorrah and its surrounding cities (Genesis 19:28-29). God is the giver and taker of life. He is the creator and has every right to create life or destroy it.

When we sit back and look, there does seem to be a contrast between the Old and New Testaments. Why is that? Are they different gods? Marcion seemed to think so. This second-century gnostic looked at both testaments and concluded that the Old Testament god was a god of anger and wrath and that the New Testament god was a god of love and mercy. Two separate gods. But he was dead wrong.

Both testaments deal with the same God. They just deal with two parts of His character. The Old Testament deals with God's holiness (see Leviticus 11:44; Psalm 22:3; 97:12). In order to preserve His goodness, again, He has the right to execute judgment on those who are wicked and have disobeyed Him. It was also to preserve the morality of His chosen people, the Israelites. They executed God's judgment "lest they teach you to do according to all their abominations which they have done for their gods, and you sin against the Lord your God" (Deuteronomy 20:18). He had to keep them holy and set apart so that the Messiah could come through their bloodline.

In contrast, we now live in the New Testament era. This one deals with His love and mercy (John 3:16; 1 John 4:8). We sinned against the one and only holy God and we deserve His punishment. However, because of His lovingkindness, He doesn't delight in anyone perishing (Ezekiel 33:11; 2 Peter 3:9). That's the reason He sent His Son to die in our place. Only when we accept that sacrifice and cleanse ourselves in Jesus' blood, are we justified before God. This is the gospel of our Lord Jesus Christ.

There is a reason God does things the way He does. We must remember that His ways are not our ways (Isaiah 55:8). We can't see what He sees, but we know it will all work out in the end to those that love Him (Romans 8:28).

This ties into His commandments as well. Skeptics will try and throw you off by asking how God could kill people but command us not to kill. First, killing is a little different than murdering. God did not murder anyone. He was just in taking those lives because they were wicked. Second, His commandments are for us, not Him. They're to keep us safe, just like any loving parent would. If I set a rule for my child to not go into my bedroom, that doesn't mean I can't go into my own bedroom. The rules are for the purpose of training the child, not the parent, or in this case, God.

To conclude, again, we must remember that the Bible doesn't condone any of these horrendous things just because it mentions it. This is an absurd notion by ignorant people. In order to draw a logical conclusion, we must come to the text without any presuppositions and simply read it as it was intended to be read.

"Christianity Was Copied from Past Religions"

One misunderstanding I hear over and over again is that Christianity is just a copy of past beliefs and religions. The Egyptians had their gods, the Romans had theirs, and the Greeks had theirs as well. The story of Jesus is no different, right? Some have even made movies about how the story of Jesus compares with many of the stories from other ancient gods. The truth is, *though, that they* made the whole thing up. It was completely fictitious. In fact, the only place you'll find these comparison "lists" of Jesus and other religions, is places that are anti-Christian, trying to sell you this heap of junk.

Even if you knew nothing about the gods of ancient civilizations, you could prove this accusation wrong. The quickest and simplest of studies can be done to show the invalidity of this claim. It was made popular by an online movie which listed many of these ancient deities, so let me take you through them to show you what I'm talking about.

Horus might be the most well-known of these gods. He was the Egyptian god that was depicted with a human body and the head of a falcon. His "eye" is also very popular to this day. In order to discredit Jesus, these are the claims that have been attributed to this Egyptian deity:

- Born on December 25th to a virgin
- A star in the East proclaimed his arrival
- Three kings came to greet the newborn "savior"
- He became a prodigious teacher at the age of 12
- At age 30, he was "baptized" and began a "ministry"

- He had twelve "disciples"; one of which betrayed him
- He was crucified, buried and rose again the third day

Now, if a babe in Christ were to look at these, they would no doubt get discouraged to move ahead in their faith in the Lord. However, let us look at each one of these claims. As I dug deeper, I found that not only was Horas *not* born on the 25th, but that he wasn't even born in December. According to the legend, he was born in the month of Khoiak, which is around the beginning of our November. This doesn't even really help the case since the Bible never says that Jesus was born on December 25th either. Although some scholars do believe Isis (his mother) to be a virgin, she was married to the god Osiris, so the chances of her still being a virgin after marriage are slim. Also, there is no "star" that proclaims the arrival of Horus, nor are there any kings that come to visit him. This also fails because kings didn't come to see Jesus either, they were wise men. And it doesn't say how many there were either. Clearly these people were going off of Christmas tradition, rather than the Sacred Text itself. In reviewing also, the word "savior" was not attributed to Horus during any part of his life. He actually never saved anyone. Too, nowhere in his story did he become a teacher at age 12 either.

Now, there is no way he could have been baptized seeing as the ritual didn't come into existence until Christianity was born and the word didn't come about until the Greek era. If you want to go back into Judaism, they had a cleaning ritual of purification and some say this is where the idea started, but this is still after Horus' time. Nowhere in his stories did he have a ministry either, seeing this too is a Christian term. Although he did have some semi-god and human followers, no account puts the number 12 in there, nor do any of them betray Horus. Last, but not least, Horus is never said to be crucified, much less raised up in three days. Most accounts put Horus at 3,000 B.C., which predates the invention of crucifixion by over two millennia. I think these skeptics need to get their history straight. As you can see, Jesus had very little, if anything, in common with Horus.[1]

Attis was the vegetation god of Phyrgia (modern day Turkey) and also later worshiped by the Greeks for a while. This was said to be around 1200 B.C. I did not find much on Attis, but just like other gods, depending on the civilization will determine which story you get. Most of these have multiple versions of multiple stories, but these are the claims that are attributed to Attis:

- Born of a virgin on December 25th
- Was crucified
- Was dead for three days
- Then resurrected

Now, let it be known that the earliest texts that we have of Attis is in the post-Christian era, so these claims most likely have been influenced by Christianity. Again, we shouldn't have to talk about the December 25th birth, since it bears no resemblance to Jesus. Actually, none of the stories of At-

---

[1] https://en.wikipedia.org/wiki/Horus
http://www.egyptianmyths.net/horus.htm

tis give any birth date. His mother is said to be Nana, but none of the stories ever call her a virgin. The only thing these two have in common is a "miraculous birth." The Holy Spirit came unto Mary, but Attis was conceived while Nana picked up a piece of fruit from an almond tree that contained one of Agdistis' castrated organs. There are many versions of Attis' death but none of them say he was crucified, which again even post-dates this deity. The most popular story was is he committed suicide, also castrating himself. Another says that Zeus was jealous of him and he sent a boar to slay Attis. The closest thing I can find to a "resurrection" is that after Attis committed suicide, his father asked Zeus to resuscitate him, but he only lets his hair grow. This resurrection claim is said to have come after Christ, so again, it was most likely influenced by it.[2]

Krishna is different from the other gods on this list for a couple of reasons. First, he is one of the only ones still being worshiped to this day, and second, unlike all of the

---

[2] greekmythology.com/Myths/Mortals/Attis/attis.html
https://greekgodsandgoddesses.net/gods/attis/

many Greek gods on this list, he doesn't have multiple versions of multiple stories of his life, which makes this study a lot easier. Krishna is the god of Hinduism. Many of you have probably known or have seen pictures of Krishna as he is depicted with blue skin. He is usually playing a flute, too. He is said to be the Avatar (prophet) of Vishnu. These are the claims made about Krishna in order to match those of Jesus:

- A star in the East proclaimed his arrival
- Was born of a virgin
- He performed miracles
- He was resurrected

I was able to obtain three different sources on Krishna's birth, and to my convenience, they all said the same thing and none of them have a star of any kind proclaiming his birth. He was the eighth child born to princess Devaki and King Vasudev. Their first seven children were slaughtered by Devaki's brother Kansa because he feared that they might kill him. However, Vasudev managed to flee the wrath of Kansa with Krishna. I shouldn't have to say much more, because being the eighth child, his mother certainly wasn't a virgin.

It is said that Krishna did perform miracles, however when the miracles of the two are compared, Krishna's seem a lot more farfetched. Just a couple that were performed by him: lifting up a mountain for seven days, multiplying himself on numerous occasions, transforming himself into other people and things, and stopping the sun for a day. Yes, Christ calmed a storm and made wine from water, but these are a little more reasonable. Christ's miracles were also performed for a reason as well. It was to show that He was "not of this world." That He was sent by God and to proclaim His name. Krishna is said to have played tricks on people with his miracles. It is also said it may have been for lesson-learning, however Jesus was more serious in nature. Also, throughout Krishna's life he is said to have killed many "bad guys," so to speak. All of these enemies were sent out to kill the lord and in turn, he would kill them, thus making "good" conquer "evil." Sounds more like a moral fairytale than a historical event.

Lastly, we come to the death of Krishna. It is said that all of his ancestors, living at the time of this event, had killed themselves with arrows while being drunk. It was just him and his brother left. They go into the woods and his brother dies, so Krishna goes to meditate on this. While meditating, a hunter mistook the lord for a deer and shoots an arrow into the lord's foot. He is said to have died immediately after this. But Jesus was whipped, scourged, had a crown of thorns jammed into His head, and was nailed to a cross, and He didn't die until much later. I think there is a difference there. Krishna's death also seems to be an accident, but I could be wrong. Jesus' death was foretold by Himself (Matthew 20:17-19) and was even prophesied long before He was born (Isaiah 53; Psalm 16:7-11). As you can see, there are many differences between the two.[3]

---

[3] https://www.ancient.eu/Krishna/
https://www.thoughtco.com/who-is-krishna-1770452

Dionysus was the Greek god of wine and ecstasy. He was mostly worshiped by the Greeks and Cretans. He was also worshiped by the Romans, but they called him Bacchus. There are a couple of different stories of him, but they mostly stayed along the same basis. Upon reading them, one may see some similarities between him and Jesus. These are the things that are attributed to Dionysus.

- Born of a virgin on December 25th
- Performed miracles
- was called the "King of Kings" and "Alpha and Omega"
- Was resurrected

In all of the stories that were read, it says that his mother Semele was a mortal, but nowhere called a virgin. Zeus was madly in love with her so he bore a child with her. Scripture makes it clear that Mary was a virgin. Being tricked by Zeus' wife, Semele asked Zeus to show his true form to her, but her being mortal couldn't see him so she burned ashes while still pregnant with Dionysus. Zeus still wanted his son to live though the incident, so he stitched the fetus to his thigh until it was born. I also never saw anything about December 25th, but we've already established that not even Jesus was born on this day.

During his life, Dionysus would teach people how to make wine and pretty much get drunk. All of his followers "worshiped" him in the styles of partying and drunken festivals out in the woods where they would take part in unrestrained sexuality and sometimes get supernatural powers of being able to rip animals (and some humans) apart with their bare hands. It never used the word "miracle," but most of them, done by Dionysus, were creating vines to make more wine or disguising himself as different people and things for no apparent reasons. He did however, manage to trick the god of the dead into bringing his mother back to life. I guess this could be a similarity between the two as it was sort of a "resurrection."

Nowhere did I read of him being called either "King of Kings" or "Alpha and Omega." The closest thing I saw was his father, Zeus, being called "the king of the gods." In ancient mythology, Zeus was the head over all other gods. Makes me wonder where people come up with these things.

In my research also, it never mentioned Dionysus resurrecting. In fact, I can't even find where he even died. The closest thing I found was someone said that he died in order to become a Greek god, which then, he would never die. I failed to see where this "death" took place though. Jesus was clearly beaten and crucified in front of many witnesses. This is an obvious difference.

In conclusion, this is the first deity that I have seen some kind of similarities with Jesus, but upon further study, it seems that Jesus is unique in His own.[4]

Mithra was the Persian god of covenant and oath. When talking to a non-believer in Christ, Mithra will probably be the most common choice of gods that come up to be compared to Jesus. They will ask why we believe in a god that is similar to a god that came after it.

---

[4] https://en.wikipedia.org/wiki/Dionysus greekmythology.com/Other_Gods/Dionysus/dionysus.html

A Quite Misunderstood Religion

There is actually not much written on Mithra. So little that you'll often hear his religion known as the "Mithra/Mithras Mysteries." With such little on him, it's amazing to see how he can be compared to Jesus, but here are the things that are attributed to him:

- Virgin birth on December 25th
- Had 12 disciples
- Performed miracles
- Was dead for three days
- Was resurrected on a Sunday

To reiterate, not much was found on Mithra, but what I did find will be presented. There is great secrecy of this religion, that's the first big difference right there. The church became very widespread when it first started out and is obviously still being preached today. The only thing I could find about his birth was one story said that he was formed out of a cave or piece of rock. It's hard to have a virgin birth here if it wasn't even human. One thing I have heard is that the Catholic Church did pick up the "December 25th birth" of Jesus from this religion. However, that point is moot since we don't know when either of them were actually born. I also didn't find anything about him having 12 disciples. Mithra was said to have had many armies though.

I did not find any miracles performed by Mithra. The most well-known image of him depicts him slaying a white bull. This is not said to be miraculous, though. When he sacrificed this bull, the Roman monuments say that it was transformed into the moon.

I apologize for the lack of material for this god but as I stated, there isn't much to research seeing as this religion was held in privacy. There is nothing said of his death, let alone for three days, and you won't find anything on him being resurrected either.

Folks, I urge you to study these things yourselves and seek the truth for yourselves. As you can plainly see, Christianity could not have been collected from these past gods, for they have little to nothing in common. The Resurrection was not taken as normality, as we can see in Acts 17:32. Still, to this day, the idea of raising from the dead is seen as preposterous. Don't be fooled by eloquent speakers and elaborate movies.[5]

---

[5] https://en.wikipedia.org/wiki/Mithraism

"You Believe in a Zombie!"

I've only heard this quote in the title a couple of times but I know that there are quite a few people that believe it. What they are referring to is the resurrection, of course. In today's society, when the dead come back to life, it's depicted as a rotten, disheveled carcass that we call a "zombie." There have been countless movies and television shows that have turned zombies into a cultural icon. Thus, unbelievers will say that Christians believe that Jesus, and others in the Bible, were "zombies." Nothing could be further from the truth.

Before I tackle the resurrection, many of these unbelievers don't even believe Jesus of Nazareth existed in the first place. This is actually a fairly new belief and it's more of a rescuing device than anything. What better way to not believe in someone than to just question their existence to begin with. It's just absurd.

There are plenty of websites that go through reasons why we should believe Jesus existed. There are many references from both Christian and non-Christian sources.[6] There are plenty of Christians' writings from both inside and outside of the Bible. Plenty of people saw Him and several wrote down their experiences. From the non-believing side, there are references—from Jewish ones like Josephus and the Babylonian Talmud to Greek and Roman references of Pliny the Younger, Tacitus, and Lucian. Suffice it to say, there was a man named Jesus that lived

---

[6] Not believing in Jesus' existence is a fairly new belief. Since His death, very few people questioned it. If you want to look up evidence for Jesus, websites such as Focus Press, Apologetics Press, and Answers in Genesis can give you some answers.

nearly two thousand years ago. It really boils down to what you believe about Him.

My point in this section is not to provide evidence that Jesus existed but that Christians don't believe in a zombie. I want to provide evidence that He, in fact, resurrected three days after He died. To show that there are legitimate reasons to believe in this historical event.

Firstly, we can believe it because it was recorded for us. The writers listed above, and plenty more, wrote down that He rose from the dead. And He wasn't a mangled or rotting corpse as He was walking around, as we would normally picture the "walking dead." He looked how He did before He died.

The Bible records five authors stating that Jesus rose from the dead. They are Matthew, Mark, Luke, John, and Paul. In addition, they were telling people all over the known world. Those against Christianity would often tell the believers not to teach about Jesus. Much of them would suffer great persecution and even be put to death.

If these people were lying about this whole thing, why would they go to their death to try and persuade others?

Secondly, the tomb was empty. The place He was buried was empty when others found it. This may not be as convincing to some, but evidence is evidence and we have to examine any and all of it.

There are typically three objections to this evidence and none of them really hold any merit. These are just ways to explain it away, but further examining it, you'll see that they aren't reasonable. Some people will say that Jesus didn't even die. That He only appeared dead but then escaped once He gained consciousness. This doesn't even make sense as multiple sources, within the Bible and out, affirm that He did die. The Bible says that the soldier pierced His side and blood and water poured out (John 19:34). This wasn't some poke in the ribcage to see if He was really dead but a piercing, most likely into the heart, to show that He was without life. Another was Josephus in his book *'Antiquities'* showing that He died under Pontius Pilate (Ant. 18.63-64). It was well known that Jesus did in fact die and wasn't faking it.

Others might claim that the followers of Jesus simply went to the wrong tomb. I've only heard of this one secondhand but you have to wonder where they came up with it. The Bible indicates that the women at the tomb knew exactly where they were. It was even said to be a new tomb (Matthew 27:60) which means it was unlikely to have been mistaken for a different one. This one seems to be the most ridiculous.

Thirdly, is that skeptics will say Jesus' body was stolen from His tomb. This might be the objection you'll hear most often. Could this be true though? Upon further investigation, we can see not. There are really only three options of who the thief could be here.

The first one would be His own disciples. That way they could try and prove that Jesus resurrected. This doesn't make sense, as I stated earlier, these followers often went through persecution. Why would someone go to their death for something they knew to be false? And further, the apostle Paul states in his first letter to the Corinthians that if Jesus didn't rise from the dead and there is no resurrection, then everything we believe and hold to and preach is futile. It's all in vain (15:12-19).

Another option would be Jesus' enemies. That way they could parade around the streets, displaying the body to the public and desecrating it in front of the people as most ancient civilizations did. This, too, is quite odd because it's not what the evidence reveals. The Jewish leaders were as shocked as anyone to learn from the guards that the tomb was empty. And when they heard it, they bribed the guards to tell people that the body was stolen (Matthew 28:11-15). Had the body been stolen by Jesus' enemies, they would have produced it and stopped the talk of resurrection right in its tracks.

The final option would be that just plain ol' grave robbers took the body. They just happened to stumble upon the tomb and take the body for fun. This might be the most preposterous option of all because when you think of robbers, they're usually after things of value that they can resell. Jesus didn't have anything but His grave wrappings in the tomb (John 20:5-7). Thieves also like to make things as easy as possible, and something that quashes each one of these, that I haven't brought up yet, is that the tomb was sealed and guarded. It would have been extremely difficult to get in—for thieves or the disciples—without being detected. And no thief would have unwrapped the body and folded the cloths before taking the body.

The only logical explanation for the tomb being empty is that God raised His Son from the dead to show that He has power over the grave. This is exactly what Jesus prophesied while He teaching His disciples (John 2:19; cf. Matthew 27:63). That's the reason they sealed the tomb in the first place!

And no, He wasn't a zombie. He appeared normally to numerous people after He resurrected. Even up to five hundred people at one time (1 Corinthians 15:6). And not one of His disciples was afraid of Him. They ate and talked with Him as though He was really there in the flesh. And they told others what they witnessed and others started believing it as well. That's how Christianity exploded into the known world. It was all because of the resurrection.

"Christians Are Too Judgmental"

John 3:16 is possibly the most known Bible verse in the world. It's so popular that many people who have never even read the Bible can quote it. It's just everywhere.

The second most popular might have to be Matthew 7:1. It is also used by people who don't read the Bible. It says, *"judge not, that you be not judged."* It is most commonly quoted by those who feel they are being attacked when a follower of Jesus tells them they are doing something wrong. In their eyes, the Bible is saying that we are not allowed to judge what people do. Is this what the Bible is actually saying though?

As always, context is key when we read something, and this is one of those cases where a verse is usually taken out of context. Keep in mind, when the Bible was written, it wasn't broken up into verses. The context of Matthew 7:1 actually goes down through verse five. Here, Jesus says, *"Judge not, that you be not judged. For with what judgment you judge, you will be judged; and with the measure you use, it will be measured back to you. And why do you look at the speck in your brother's eye, but do not consider the plank in your own eye? Or how can you say to your brother, 'Let me remove the speck from your eye'; and look, a plank is in your own eye? Hypocrite! First remove the plank from your own eye, and then you will see clearly to remove the speck from your brother's eye."*

Does reading it in context give the first verse a new meaning? It should. Here, Jesus isn't talking about all judging. He is talking about hypocritical judging. He is saying that we shouldn't judge someone for something they're doing when we are doing the exact same thing—or worse.

In fact, Jesus condemns hypocrisy a lot. It might just be the one sin He talks about the most. Many times, Jesus speaks out against the Pharisees for saying one thing but doing another. We aren't to deceive people

This also goes along the lines of James 4:11-12. It states, *"Do not speak evil of one another, brethren. He who speaks evil of a brother and judges his brother, speaks evil of the law and judges the law. But if you judge the law, you are not a doer of the law but a judge. There is one Lawgiver, who is able to save and to destroy. Who are you to judge another?"* Here, James is talking about slandering or insulting someone. This, along with hypocritical judgment would be wrong. We have no right to pass such judgment.

Now, contrary to popular belief, not all judging is sinful. I can't speak for every Christian out there because I know of Christians that use hypocritical judgment. It's sad to see, for sure. I can only tell you that we are to judge, but we are to do it properly.

While there is judging that is condemned, there is also judgment that we are commanded to do. Check out John 7:24 which says, *"Do not judge according to appearance, but judge with righteous judgment."* Yes, there is a right way for Christians to judge and that's to do it righteously. This means to do it according to God's standards. To use the Bible as our rule of thumb. Using our own judgments make it hypocritical because we are all human and imperfect, but speaking on behalf of God makes our judgment righteous.

I cringe when I hear "Christians" today doing things like street preaching and protesting things. This is how *not* to judge. Every time I hear them, I think to myself that simple cliché question, "what would Jesus do?" Jesus most certainly wouldn't do that. Aside from the Pharisees, Jesus never called people out on their sin publicly, yelling obscenities and name calling, telling people they are going to Hell, etc. He talked with sinners one-on-one, politely and in a loving manner, informing them that they had sin in their lives and they needed forgiveness from

God. And the only reason He called out the Pharisees was because they were being hypocritical. The worst way to preach the gospel is yelling in sinners faces.

It does make me laugh a little, but it is incredibly sad to hear people say "only God can judge me." While this is a highly valid statement, we shouldn't wait for God to be our judge because then it will be too late. We are to heed the warnings of His people, that way we can be judged by what Jesus did, not ourselves. And if you think about it, when a Christian tells you to repent of sin, *that is* basically God judging you. Just don't wait until the final judgment.

This is one of those things that I believe the church can do a better job at. Many nowadays have leaned toward this "judgmental" side and just don't care how they come across. When we judge righteously, it means to do it with love (cf. Ephesians 4:15). We ought to understand that the lost are people too. They have a soul, just like us. We need to be more understanding of their story and worldview. Once the respect is there, they are more likely to listen to what we have to say and that they are in need of a Savior, too. This is the best way, in my opinion, to evangelize and judge to the lost.

"Most Wars Have Been Fought in the Name of Religion"

Okay, this one isn't geared directly towards Christianity per se, but religion in general. For me personally, I have only heard this one a few times, but I've seen it in many forums and other places. This accusation has been around now for a while. Some people will make this assumption that the numerous wars mankind has had in the past have been started over religion. This is just simply not true. I can only assume that the ones that make this claim just use it as a rescuing device and haven't actually done their research. Let us examine the data, shall we?

The death tolls on a select number of wars have caused some to shy away from Christianity. The Crusades is usually the biggest one brought up when discussing this topic. It is used by many skeptics to say religion is bad because it kills people "in the name of God." There have actually been multiple 'Crusades,' but the one they're usually referring to is the one against the Muslims over the Holy Land, and this war killed roughly 1-3 million people.[7] That's about the same as the Vietnam War. The Crusades lasted about 200 years. In 1994, in Rwanda, it only took 100 days to kill one million people. Also, most people think that this war was only against Muslims, but it wasn't. There were others among the number, too. This included other Christians.

The Crusades isn't even the deadliest Christian war as it's made out to be. It's probably third on the list. The first was a war in central Europe called the Thirty Years' War. (It was actually just shy of thirty years, but who's counting). This war was

---

[7] Each death toll stat can be found at https://en.wikipedia.org/wiki/List_of_wars_by_death_toll

between the Catholics and the Protestants in the Holy Roman Empire. Around 8 million people were killed. Some say as much as 11 million.

In second place was another war just prior to the Thirty Years' War in France. Around 2-4 million people were killed. This one as well was between the Catholics and Protestants. Yes, it is said that religion was the reason these wars started, but it became much more politically driven as time went on.

Now, these are just three 'Christian' wars. Have there been any that *weren't* religious in nature? Just looking at American history alone, I can name the Revolutionary War, Civil War, World Wars I & II, Korean War, and Vietnam War. That's six wars right there and none of them originated over religion. Like most wars, they started over power.

So, this brings us to nine wars in total. If we're still concluding that the first three were started over religion, that's only 33%. And if we were to compare the death tolls, on the high end, even taking into account soldiers that died of famine and disease and such during the war, at most, we're only at about 15% dead. Clearly, we can see that it's just not the case that "most wars are started over religion." However, let's take it a bit further.

This was just a look at the history of the United States. The People's Republic of China has had five wars that have killed over twenty million people each in their lifetime. They had the Three Kingdoms War, the An Lushan Rebellion, and the Second Sino-Japanese War, just to name a few. None of these were started over religion, but over power over land and influence. This brings us down to 21% of the ones I've mentioned.

There were also a few wars that were fought in Eurasia, at the time, that have had many casualties as well. The Mongol Conquests and the conquests of Timur had upwards of 40 million and 25 million deaths, respectively. These were also conquests over territory and not in the name of religion.

This drops us to 19%. Do you see now how futile this accusation is?

Now, there were a number of Muslim wars who many claim were in the name of religion; however, they were mostly to conquer more territory. Even if we were to count these though, the number is still minute in comparison to the total number of wars that mankind has been involved in. In fact, the number ends up being less than 7% of wars that had religion as the agitator.[8] As I stated, the vast majority were caused by political ambition or to conquer more land and possessions. It's usually when one side feared the other side would gain more that most wars started.

When we listen to our own will and are caught up in our own desires, we get into trouble. That is when things get ugly, when we start coveting things that others have. Let us submit to God's will and see how truly beautiful life can be when we love each other as God loves us.

---

[8] http://www.blogos.org/compellingtruth/does-religion-cause-war.php

"The Church"

What is the Church?

There are several misconceptions about the church. I'd like to discuss three of them that I hear most often. Suppose I was to ask you, "how was church last week?" What would you be thinking then? In today's society, the word *church* has several different meanings. It could mean the act of worship at a specific time, it could mean a corporate religious structure/denomination, or it could mean the place of worship or building itself. What if I were to tell you that these are mistaken? What are you thinking now? While it is true that this is how our English word *church* is used, I'm going to be talking about what the Bible says about the church.

I always start by defining my terms. In the New Testament, the Greek word for church is *ekklesia*. It means "the called out," as it's derived from the two Greek words *ek* (out of) and *kaleo* (invite, call). It is a term given to Christians who have placed their faith in Jesus and been washed in His blood for the forgiveness of sins. So, *the church* actually is not the building of worship, but the people who meet at that building. *Ekklesia* can also be translated "assembly" or "congregation," but since the translators mostly used 'church,' so will I.

When we become a Christian, we are added to the church (called out; Acts 2:47). But what are we being called out from? Just as God called out the Israelites from Egypt in the Old Testament, we are now being called out of the world and its wickedness (cf. John 8:23; 15:19). We have been called to live a life of holiness before God and the world (Ephesians 1:4; 1 Peter 1:16).

The church of God started on the day of Pentecost in Acts 2. Around three thousand souls were saved that day. That's an enormous number. They heard the gospel preached to them by the Apostles. They were sorrowful and asked what they should do (v. 37). So, they were told to repent and be baptized for the remission of sins (v. 38; 3:19). This is what the church still preaches today.

Many conversions can be found throughout the book of Acts. Although it's not explicitly stated, they were all forgiven by the same formula. That's repentance and remission of sins because that's what the Apostles were told to preach (Luke 24:47). Once we've repented and cleansed ourselves of past sins, God enters us into the church.

Now, we see in Scripture that the saved go by many names. There is the "church of God" (1 Corinthians 1:2; 10:32; Galatians 1:13), "church of Christ" (Romans 16:16), "saints" (Romans 1:7; 1 Corinthians 1:2), "kingdom of God" (Matthew 21:43; Colossians 4:11), "kingdom of Christ" (Ephesians 5:5), "Christians" (Acts 11:26; 26:28; 1 Peter 4:16), "disciples" (Acts 9:1), and "body of Christ" (Romans 12:5; 1 Corinthians 12:27; Ephesians 4:12; 5:23), just to name a few. Again, this is simply the assembly of

Christians who have devoted their lives to Christ. A life that is holy and set apart for God (Romans 12:1-2). This is God's church. The people, not any building. If you have been forgiven, you are part of the church.

So, did you catch that last sentence? Read it again. If you are a Christian, you are a part of *the* church. When you read throughout the New Testament, you always see the word 'the' in front of the word 'church.' Want to take a guess why? Because there is only one. There is only one body (Ephesians 4:4) and we learned earlier that the body of Christ *is* the church of Christ, so therefore we can conclude there is only one church. The church that Jesus said He would build (Matthew 16:18) and the one "He purchased with His own blood" (Acts 20:28). He didn't say He would build *many* churches, but "*My* church." That denotes only one.

It Started with the Restoration Movement

Now, many get caught up when they see the name "church of Christ" and equate it to the American Restoration Movement that happened in the 19th century. They will say that the "church of Christ" was founded by Alexander Campbell and a few other men. However, they are mistaken. This is another common misconception about the church that I wish to clear up for you.

I won't get into it here, but there is a fascinating study you can do on the patriarchs of the Restoration Movement and I would highly recommend it. The church, though, did not start with these men. As I mentioned before, it started all the way back in Acts 2 on the day of Pentecost, back in the first century. All these patriarchs did was see the vast amount of denominations in their time and each had strayed from the Bible. They simply tried to restore the church back to its first-century roots. They wanted to keep Bible names for Bible doctrine and use it as the sole authority when it came to religious matters.

You can also look back prior to the 19th century back in Europe. There were a group of people around the 16th century called 'Anabaptists,' and a very intriguing study can be done on them as well. Like many sects, this name was used as a derogatory term by opposers as it meant "one who baptizes again." Those who were called Anabaptists believed infant baptism was unauthorized and bore no power, and thus they were rebaptizing people for the forgiveness of sins as the Bible teaches. They believed people must believe and repent *prior* to their baptism, and a baby can't do that. Baptism is for the remission of sins and babies don't have any sins. These people began to form during the Reformation Movement in the 16th century and were even called "radical reformers" because they believed the Reformation wasn't going far enough. It's really interesting, to me at least, what they believed in, which was to go back and restore the church of old.

Now, unfortunately, because they were in the minority, much of their writings haven't been preserved. A lot of what we know about them comes from the opposition. What we can see, though, is that they did believe in many of the ideas that the American restorers believed in. The main one was simply getting back to the Bible.

They didn't like all of the Christian sects and new philosophies that were arising. It seemed as though many had their own ideas about what the Bible was teaching, so they started their own little sects. This is how many denominations have started. Those in the Restoration Movement simply wanted to let the Bible speak for itself. They wanted to restore the church back to its roots. Back to when it began. They weren't trying to reform or protest the Catholic or Orthodox churches or any other denominations. They just read Scripture and used it as their sole authority.

One of the beliefs these two movements had in common was to use of "church of Christ" or any of the other names the Bible uses as the description on their signs. We can actually see evidence of many churches throughout Europe that just use "church of Christ" on their buildings. It's just what we are. Why go by any other name? I'll let you read more about the Anabaptists yourselves,[9] but suffice to say that many

---

[9] I'm not saying that the Restorationists were the Anabaptists of old. I'm merely pointing out that they had similar be-

throughout history have simply wanted to be called "Christians." That's it. If you're a Christian, you belong to Christ's church.

We Don't Need the Church

One last misconception I've heard about the church is that one doesn't need the church if they just have Christ. This is supposed to justify their belief that if you just believe in Jesus, you shouldn't have to assemble with any local congregation of the Lord's church. I'm not really sure where they get this from because I don't see it in Scripture. It's more of an appeal to those that just don't like "organized religion." (Makes me wonder if they like disorganized religion.)

Remember, we have established that *we* are the church, not the building. The Lord's church gathered every first day of the week (Acts 20:7) to do a couple of things: Worship God and edify one another. They wor-

---

liefs. For more on Anabaptists doctrine, visit anabaptists.org/history/what-is-an-anabaptist.html

For more information on going beyond the American Restoration Movement, visit traces-of-the-kingdom.org/

shiped God by doing things like singing and hearing His word and also by commemorating Christ's death in the Lord's Supper. They would edify each other by fellowshipping and giving of their means. This is the purpose of us gathering together. To say you don't need the church is just absurd. The church is the body of Christ, so that's like saying you don't need the body of Jesus, just Jesus. How does that make any sense?

If life has taught me anything, it's that we can't live it alone. Not only do we need God, but we need each other. When you don't interact with other members of the Lord's church, you're isolating yourself, which God has not commanded. How are we to evangelize to the lost if we isolate ourselves? God made us to be sociable people. We ought to be growing the kingdom of God, not separating it. The moment we think we don't need the church is the moment we need it most.

So, these are the ones I hear most often about our Lord's church. I pray that you always look to the Bible for spiritual matters and choosing the right church. When looking for a church home, you'll often hear people say something like, "I'm looking for a church that's right for me." How about looking for God's church? *His* family? If you're interested in learning about His church, I'd love to show it to you.

Conclusion

Well, I pray that you've learned something from these studies. My job isn't to make anyone a believer with this book. I'm only here to represent my faith the best way I know how.

Again, this isn't every misconception out there about Christianity. These are just the ones that I have found to be the most popular among the naysayers and unlearned. And as you can see, it didn't take a whole lot of studying to show that these accusations are false. There is truth out there.

I could have also gone into the accusation that says that science and religion are at odds with one another, but there really isn't much to write on. This also is just not true.

Many great scientists from Sir Isaac Newton to Albert Einstein believed in the Creator. They believe science actually points us towards God, not farther away from Him. Science can only take us so far though. Science can only point us to God. It doesn't tell us about Him. That's what God's word does. That book we call 'the Bible.'

It tells us that He created us and we rebelled against Him. Therefore, we are sentenced to death by a just God. It is our sin that separates us from our God (Isaiah 59:2). However, He is also a loving God and doesn't want anyone to die (Ezekiel 18:32; 2 Peter 3:9), so He has given us a way out that we may be justified in His sight. He sent His Son, Jesus, to suffer and die, essentially taking our place. That is God's gift to the world and it's by accepting that gift that we can be made right again with our Maker.

I beg you to search these things out for yourself. Don't believe everything you hear. Don't even believe everything I've said. Search it out for yourself. Truth is there waiting for you. Nowadays, truth is like your reflection in a dirty mirror. It's there. It just takes a little elbow grease to find it.

On the Day of Judgment, we will all give an account to the things we've done, whether good or bad (Romans 2:5-10; 2 Corinthians 5:10). We can either believe in that truth and accept it, or deny it. If you accept it by faith and wash away your sins before that day, you will inherit eternal life as God has promised (John 3:16, 36; 17:3; Romans 6:23; Hebrews 5:9; 10:36; 1 John 5:13).

www.ingramcontent.com/pod-product-compliance
Lightning Source LLC
Chambersburg PA
CBHW071320040426
42444CB00009B/2054